21
22.

Earthquakes and Volcanoes

LOOKING AT LANDSCAPES

Earthquakes and Volcanoes

Alison Rae

Evans

Published by Evans Brothers Limited
2A Portman Mansions
Chiltern Street
London W1U 6NR

British Library Cataloguing in Publication Data
Rae, Alison
Earthquakes and volcanoes. - (Looking at landscapes)
1. Earthquakes - Juvenile literature
2. Volcanoes - Juvenile literature
I. Title
551.2

ISBN 0237527421

Consultant: Simon Ross
Editor: Sonya Newland
Designer: Big Blu Ltd
Picture researcher: Julia Bird

Contents

Introduction

Earthquakes and volcanoes are some of the most spectacular and dangerous natural hazards on the planet – they have been occurring for millions of years and they are still happening all the time. This activity largely takes place at the boundaries where the Earth's plates meet, either colliding or grinding past one another.

Sometimes the movement of these plates causes red-hot molten rock to bubble up through the Earth's crust. Great pressure in the areas beneath the surface of the Earth forces this magma upwards in a great explosion, creating a volcano. When volcanoes erupt they can eject lava as well as dust and rock. Over time, this hardens and builds up to form layers that become part of a distinctive volcanic landscape. In other regions, the great force caused by the plates meeting makes the Earth shake, sometimes resulting in great cracks on the surface of the Earth and sending out shock waves for many kilometres.

▼ The magnificent but deadly firework displays caused by volcanoes, like this one in Iceland, are some of the most impressive features of the natural world.

▲ Earthquakes like the one that hit Mexico City in 1985 can cause severe damage and loss of life.

Some parts of the world suffer dreadfully from the effects of plate activity. Whole settlements can be destroyed and often are not rebuilt because of the emotional pain involved. When an earthquake strikes, it causes buildings and other structures to collapse, killing many people and devastating whole cities. Sometimes they can even cause tsunamis – massive waves that can sweep on to land, washing away everything in their paths. Hundreds of earthquakes are recorded by seismologists every year, but only a very few of them are severe enough to cause serious damage. When a volcano erupts, even if the lava flow poses no immediate threat, the enormous clouds of dust and ash can spread great distances and cover a region in a thick suffocating blanket. However, this can create very fertile land, which is useful for cultivation.

Despite the danger these natural hazards pose, many people still live in areas where they take place. In poorer countries, this is often because the inhabitants simply do not have the means to move to a safer region. In other parts of the world, people believe that the advantages outweigh the risks, and they are willing to stay. As technology progresses and our understanding of earthquakes and volcanoes increases, scientists are better able to predict when they may occur and to prepare for the disaster they may cause. Whatever measures are taken, though, earthquakes and volcanic eruptions will remain a constant reminder of the immense power of natural forces on our planet.

▼ Scientists study these natural phenomena in the hope of predicting when and where an eruption or earthquake is likely to occur. Here, a scientist takes a measurement of lava flow on La Fournaise volcano in the Indian Ocean.

What Causes Earthquakes and Volcanoes?

If we could dig through the surface of the Earth to its centre, we would see that it has four layers.

The Earth's core – inner and outer together – has a diameter of nearly 3,500 km and is larger than our neighbouring planet, Mars. The temperature of the Earth's core is about 6,200°C – hotter even than the surface of the Sun. Towards the surface of the Earth temperatures decrease, but even the lower parts of the crust can be as hot as 1,200°C. The surface of the Earth is characterised by a series of gigantic 'plates', of different sizes and shapes. Because the Earth's plates actually move in relation to each other, a great deal of activity takes place at their boundaries or margins.

The Earth's crust

The thickness of the Earth's crust relative to the rest of the planet has been described in a number of ways: it is as thin as the skin of an apple compared to the rest of the fruit, or it is like a postage stamp stuck on to a football. The crust is of two types – oceanic and continental. Oceanic crust forms the sea bed and is made of a dense rock called basalt. Continental crust sits on top of some of the oceanic crust. Up to 80 km thick, it is made up of less dense rocks such as granite.

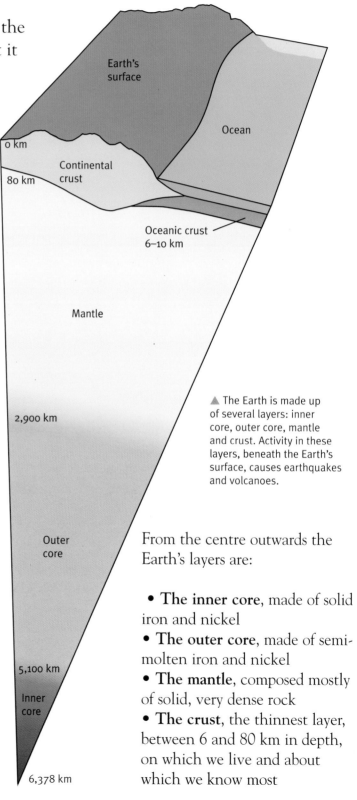

▲ The Earth is made up of several layers: inner core, outer core, mantle and crust. Activity in these layers, beneath the Earth's surface, causes earthquakes and volcanoes.

From the centre outwards the Earth's layers are:

- **The inner core**, made of solid iron and nickel
- **The outer core**, made of semi-molten iron and nickel
- **The mantle**, composed mostly of solid, very dense rock
- **The crust**, the thinnest layer, between 6 and 80 km in depth, on which we live and about which we know most

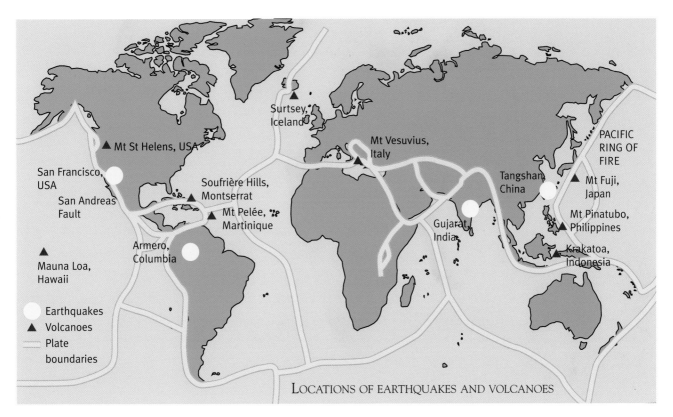

Map labels:
- Surtsey, Iceland
- Mt St Helens, USA
- San Francisco, USA
- San Andreas Fault
- Soufrière Hills, Montserrat
- Mt Pelée, Martinique
- Mauna Loa, Hawaii
- Armero, Columbia
- Mt Vesuvius, Italy
- Tangshan, China
- Gujarat, India
- PACIFIC RING OF FIRE
- Mt Fuji, Japan
- Mt Pinatubo, Philippines
- Krakatoa, Indonesia

Legend:
- Earthquakes
- Volcanoes
- Plate boundaries

LOCATIONS OF EARTHQUAKES AND VOLCANOES

Plate tectonics

Plate tectonics is a theory, developed in the 1960s, about the Earth's plates – how they were formed, how they move, and the results of their movements. The most dramatic earthquake and volcanic action happens at plate boundaries, but the precise nature of this activity depends on the direction of plate movement.

At constructive margins, plates move away from each other, magma from the mantle rises to fill the space and the solidified magma forms new crust. These constructive zones can be found beneath the oceans as enormous ridges, such as the Mid-Atlantic Ridge. Volcanoes are common at these margins. Earthquakes do occur, but they tend not to be very destructive.

At destructive boundaries, two plates move towards each other and crust is destroyed. At subduction zones, one plate is forced downwards beneath the overriding plate. As the oceanic plate subducts (moves down) below the continental plate, rising temperatures and friction cause the oceanic rocks to melt and turn into magma. Some of the magma rises to the surface through cracks in the

▲ It is easy to see a relationship between the locations of volcanoes and earthquakes, and the boundaries of the Earth's plates. However, there are a few volcanoes that exist far away from the plate margins. These are called intra-plate volcanoes and they are located over hot spots, where plumes of magma (liquid or molten rock) break through relatively thin parts of the crust.

▲ Iceland is the only part of the Mid-Atlantic Ridge that rises above sea-level, and its central volcanic plateau is erupting almost constantly.

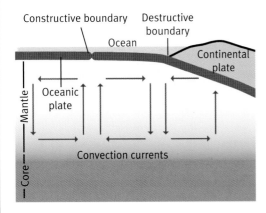

Constructive boundary
Destructive boundary
Ocean
Continental plate
Mantle
Oceanic plate
Core
Convection currents

▲ Plates move because of processes that take place within the mantle. The rocks in the mantle are not always solid. Pressure increases with depth and this in turn leads to an increase in temperature. At certain depths, the rock of the mantle reaches its melting point and magma is produced. This then rises towards the surface, from high pressure deep down to relatively low pressure towards the surface. Scientists believe that there are circular currents of heat called convection currents operating within the mantle, which are responsible for the movement of the plates.

▶ At constructive boundaries, two plates move away from each other and volcanoes often occur.

▶ At destructive boundaries one plate can override another, forming a subduction zone, where earthquakes can occur as the plates stick to each other, then jolt free.

▶ Another feature of destructive boundaries is an island arc – chains of underwater volcanoes formed by the subducted plate melting and forming magma.

continental plate, forming volcanoes with sometimes explosive activity. As the two plates slide past and over each other, substantial friction stores energy within the rocks. The plates can become stuck and the jolt experienced on the surface of the Earth when they finally pull apart is an earthquake.

Two continental plates moving towards each other cause earthquakes but not volcanoes. This is because the plates are relatively light and they tend to crumple rather than subduct. With no subduction, there is no formation of magma to feed volcanoes. The immense crumpling pressures push up huge mountain ranges like the Alps and the Himalayas. This type of plate margin is called a collision zone.

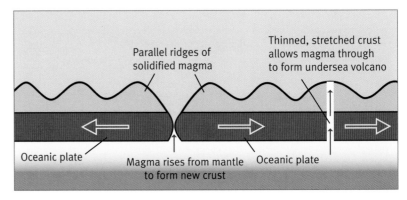

Parallel ridges of solidified magma

Thinned, stretched crust allows magma through to form undersea volcano

Oceanic plate

Magma rises from mantle to form new crust

Oceanic plate

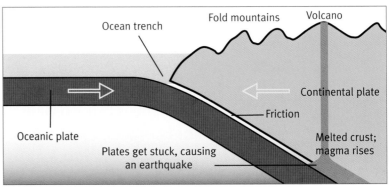

Ocean trench

Fold mountains

Volcano

Oceanic plate

Continental plate

Friction

Melted crust; magma rises

Plates get stuck, causing an earthquake

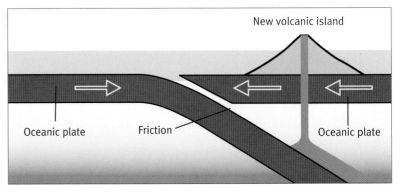

New volcanic island

Oceanic plate

Friction

Oceanic plate

Fault lines

A fault is a crack in the rocks of the Earth's crust, where one section of rock has moved relative to the other. Faulting is caused by plate movement and can be either vertical or horizontal.

Faults that move rocks horizontally form another type of plate margin, known as a conservative boundary. These are different from all others because the two plates move alongside each other rather than moving towards or away from each other. No new crust is formed and no existing crust is destroyed. There is no volcanic activity, but it is along fault lines that earthquakes most frequently occur.

▶ At a conservative plate margin, friction is generated and energy stored as the rocks along the edges of the plates move past each other. In the same way as at destructive boundaries, sometimes the two sides become stuck and only a severe jolt can shake them loose. Shock waves called seismic waves spread out in all directions. It is this sudden jolt or release of pressure that causes an earthquake.

▲ The Great Rift Valley in East Africa is a different kind of fault line. Some scientists think it is a new constructive plate margin just about to open up. This huge valley is 5,000 km long and in places it is over 1 km deep. It contains volcanoes such as Mount Kilimanjaro in Tanzania, now thought to be extinct. At 5,895 metres, it is the highest mountain in Africa.

⬤ The San Andreas Fault

The most famous fault in the world, the San Andreas Fault, causes earthquakes in one of America's richest and most densely populated urban areas. Stretching right through California and southwards into Mexico, it is 1,125 km long. The San Andreas Fault is unusual, however, because the plates on either side of it, the Pacific and the North American, are not moving in opposite directions. Instead, both are moving approximately north-westwards, but they are doing so at different speeds (6 cm per year for the Pacific plate and 1 cm per year for the North American plate).

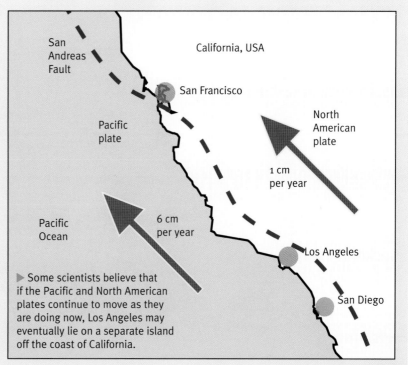

San Andreas Fault

California, USA

San Francisco

Pacific plate

North American plate

1 cm per year

Pacific Ocean

6 cm per year

Los Angeles

San Diego

▶ Some scientists believe that if the Pacific and North American plates continue to move as they are doing now, Los Angeles may eventually lie on a separate island off the coast of California.

The Quaking Earth

Earthquakes occur at all types of plate margin; however, they tend to be most powerful where huge pressures build up, such as at destructive and conservative plate margins, and at collision zones. With the exception of Antarctica, all continents experience earthquakes. When an earthquake occurs, a shock or jolt takes place at a point underground known as the focus. The energy spreads out from the focus as a series of seismic or shock waves. These are most powerful immediately around the focus and become weaker with distance. The point on the Earth's surface vertically above the focus is the epicentre. People living here usually feel the maximum force of the earthquake's energy.

▲ This seismograph records the waves caused by the earthquake that hit Afghanistan in March 2002. These readings were taken thousands of miles away in Edinburgh, Scotland. The seismic waves took about 15 minutes to travel through the Earth from Afghanistan to Scotland.

▶ The two main types of earthquake wave are P waves and S waves. S waves move from side to side. P waves move forward through the Earth like a coiled spring.

Seismic waves

Three different types of earthquake wave exist: P waves (primary or 'push' waves); S waves (secondary or 'shake' waves); and L waves (longitudinal or 'surface' waves). Both P and S waves start at the focus, but they move in different ways. P waves move like a 'slinky' toy; energy pulses forwards from the focus. S waves behave more like a rope being waved from one end, shaking the ground back and forth. L waves are very complex waves that move close to the surface. They have high amplitudes and can be very destructive to property.

P wave

S wave

Each type of wave travels at a different speed. P waves are the fastest and L the slowest. On a seismogram (a graph showing the pattern of earthquake waves) the P waves are drawn first, because they move more quickly. Scientists can work out how far away the focus of an earthquake is by recording the time difference between when P and S waves reach a particular point away from the earthquake. P waves travel through solids and liquids alike, but S waves will not pass through liquids. This means they bounce off Earth's liquid inner core. From careful measurement of this behaviour scientists have worked out the size and composition of the layers of our planet.

In a few earthquakes, seismic waves have behaved unusually because of the physical geography of the area. Mexico City suffered very severely when an earthquake hit in 1985, yet it was far from the epicentre and should have been fairly safe. The city is built on an old lake bed made of soft sediments. The seismic waves made the ground wobble like a jelly, causing many buildings to collapse or simply sink into the soft ground. Only a small part of the city is built on solid rock. Today this area is much in demand and has the highest house prices.

▲ The Mexico City earthquake in 1985 caused hundreds of buildings to collapse, killing or injuring thousands of people.

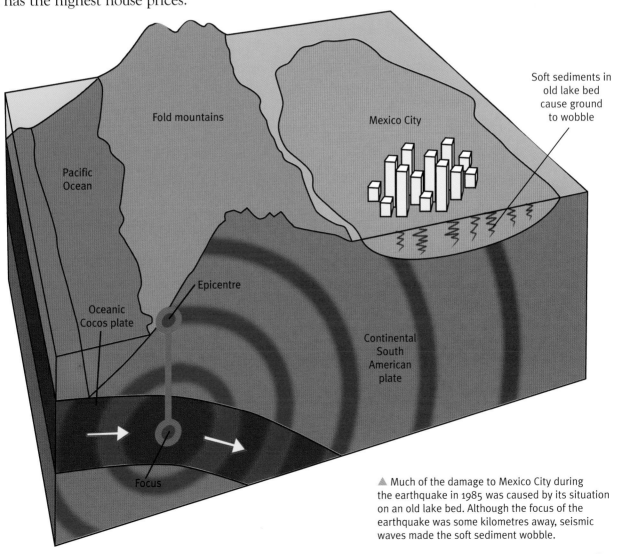

Soft sediments in old lake bed cause ground to wobble

Fold mountains

Mexico City

Pacific Ocean

Epicentre

Oceanic Cocos plate

Continental South American plate

Focus

▲ Much of the damage to Mexico City during the earthquake in 1985 was caused by its situation on an old lake bed. Although the focus of the earthquake was some kilometres away, seismic waves made the soft sediment wobble.

In December 2003, an earthquake measuring 6.6 on the Richter scale hit the city of Bam in Iran. It also measured high on the Mercalli scale – 70 per cent of the city was destroyed.

Charles Richter, who devised the scale that is named after him, pictured here with his seismograph.

Measuring earthquakes

The Richter scale is the most common scale for measuring the magnitude of earthquakes. It is a logarithmic scale, which means that each point is ten times greater than the one below it. Thus, a magnitude 7 earthquake is 10 times larger than one of magnitude 6, 100 times larger than magnitude 5 and 1,000 times larger than magnitude 4. This is an open-ended scale, since it is based on measurements not descriptions. Major world earthquakes usually measure 6.0 or higher on the Richter scale.

The Mercalli scale examines the effects of the event, i.e. how much damage is done. This scale does not need instruments to measure it; it can all be done by observation. The Mercalli scale has 12 intensity ratings:

I People do not feel any movement.
II When standing still or on the upper floors of tall buildings a slight movement might be noticed.
III Hanging objects swing back and forward.

IV Dishes, windows and doors rattle. Parked cars rock.

V Sleeping people wake up. Doors swing, liquids spill, trees shake.

VI People have trouble walking. Furniture moves, plaster cracks and things fall from shelves and hooks. No real structural damage yet.

VII People have difficulty standing. Moving cars shake. Loose materials fall from buildings.

VIII Drivers have trouble steering. Towers and chimneys might fall. Branches break. Poorly built buildings suffer severe damage, but well constructed ones only slight.

IX Well-constructed buildings suffer considerable damage. Underground pipes break. The ground cracks.

X Most buildings are destroyed. Dams are broken and landslides occur. Roads and railways crack or bend.

XI Most buildings and bridges collapse. Large cracks appear in the ground.

XII Almost everything is destroyed. Ground moves in waves.

▲ Seismologists use a variety of recording and timing equipment to measure seismic waves and to gauge a picture of the rock strata below the Earth's surface in earthquake-prone areas. Artificial seismic wave generators send shock waves into the Earth and any breaks in the rock strata are recorded on machines like the ones pictured. This can help warn of an impending earthquake.

◄ This aerial photograph shows the damage caused by an earthquake in California in 1994. This part of Los Angeles was over the epicentre, and the earthquake measured 6.6 on the Richter scale. At the top in the centre a department store and car park have collapsed. A train has also been derailed, blocking a road (bottom right).

Effects in different countries

The San Andreas Fault, dividing the North American and Pacific plates, is one of the best-known earthquake zones in the world. Activity here affects a More Economically Developed Country (MEDC). Severe earthquakes hit San Francisco in both 1906 and 1989, and Los Angeles in 1994.

The north-east Indian state of Gujarat is close to a collision zone, where the Indo-Australian plate meets the Eurasian plate. As a Less Economically Developed Country (LEDC), this region of India suffered severely in the 2001 earthquake.

MEDCs have the money and technology to protect themselves from many of the effects of earthquakes. LEDCs are in a much worse position. Most people can only afford quite basic homes, made from cheap materials; these can collapse easily, killing those inside.

MEDCs can also afford better-equipped and well-trained emergency services. Help reaches people more quickly. In LEDCs communications are often so poor that help is slow in coming. Earthquakes are usually such sudden events that there is no warning. In MEDCs people almost always know whether or not they live in a high-risk zone. They are educated in what to do to in the event of an earthquake. In LEDCs communications are worse and people are less aware of measures of protection.

▼ Although earthquakes – like this one that derailed a train (pictured) in Los Angeles in 1994 – can cause havoc in MEDCs, the damage and loss of life is often far less than in LEDCs, because emergency services are well-trained and communications more efficient.

⬤ The San Francisco earthquakes

The great earthquake of 1906 began at 5.12 a.m. on 18 April; the ground shook for 45 to 60 seconds. Measuring 8.25 on the Richter scale, it remains the largest event ever recorded along the San Andreas Fault. Around 700 deaths were reported, but many believe the true figure was three or four times higher.

People died or were injured in various circumstances. They were killed as buildings collapsed and by the fires that broke out over the city from fractured gas pipes. Older, wooden buildings proved more resistant to the earthquake shaking, but were at greater risk from the fires. In

▲ During the 1906 San Francisco earthquake, fires broke out across the city and burned for three days. Most of the city centre was destroyed as the fires spread.

fact, the fires caused far more destruction than the ground shaking.

The 1989 quake caused fewer deaths. Most of these were on the double-decker Cypress freeway in Oakland. Although the city was better prepared for the 1989 earthquake, as technology had improved greatly, the cost of the damage was still over $6 billion. It was America's most expensive natural disaster to date.

Warning signs

Scientific earthquake prediction is not always very accurate, but sometimes there are warning signs before an earthquake strikes. Large earthquakes release enormous amounts of energy in the form of seismic waves. Some of the energy that builds up in the Earth's crust 'leaks out' prior to the catastrophic event. The build-up of high electric fields where the rock meets the air may provide an explanation for the reported occurrences of pre-earthquake 'ground-

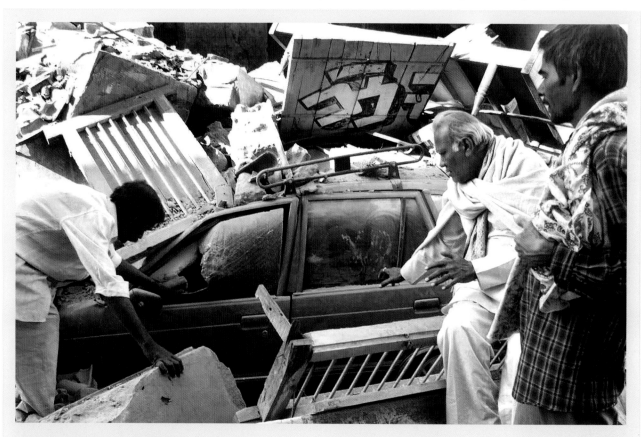

● The Bhuj earthquake

The city of Bhuj in India was almost at the epicentre of a 7.9 magnitude earthquake, which occurred on 26 January 2001. The 45-second shake caused a huge amount of damage. Places far from the epicentre were also hit badly because their buildings collapsed so easily. In Ahmedabad, 443 km from Bhuj, where the population is around five million, over 100 buildings were destroyed. Many structures were made of heavy, reinforced concrete, which is easily

▲ When the massive earthquake struck Bhuj in the Indian province of Gujarat in 2001, the city and surrounding villages suffered severely. The loss of life was more than it might have been because it was a national holiday; more people than usual were at home and were buried as their houses collapsed. These men look at a car buried under the wreckage of a collapsed building.

wrecked by shaking. Roofs were flat and made of a single section, so when they collapsed, people trapped underneath were literally buried alive. Those who survived had lost everything.

hugging fog'. Electrically charged particles in the air might explain why animals are seen to behave in a strange, agitated way before an earthquake; the particles could also be the cause of the luminous phenomena known as 'earthquake lights'. Unusual lights and sounds were reported the night before the Tangshan earthquake in 1976.

Tsunamis

Tsunamis are huge ocean waves caused by an earthquake or volcanic eruption beneath the sea. If they hit land they can cause severe damage. The extent of this depends on how far the wave has travelled before it hits land. The longer the distance, the less energy the wave has remaining; but the further the wave travels the greater its height. The shape of the coastline is also significant. Coastlines that slope gently into the sea and bays that narrow quickly inland both concentrate energy and make the waves higher and stronger, and the potential damage worse. The intensity of a tsunami is gauged by its wave height:

▲ Tsunamis can be caused by earthquakes or volcanic eruptions. This painting depicts the wave caused by the eruption of Krakatoa in 1883.

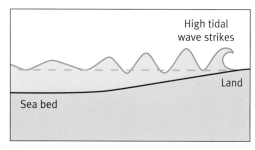

A gently sloping coast allows a tsunami to build up higher and higher.

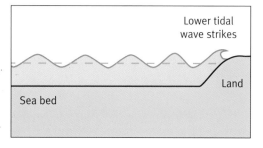

Along a steeper coast, the wave is not able to build as much as on a gentle slope.

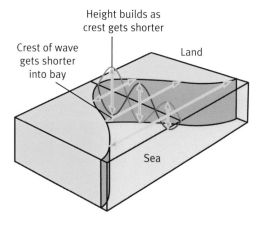

The longer the crest, the more energy there is in the wave – a bay shortens the length of the crest, so concentrates the energy, and this makes the tsunami higher and higher.

Aceh in northern Indonesia was the first inhabited area hit by the Asian tsunami in December 2004. Here, a man walks through the wreckage caused by the giant waves.

0.5 m: very slight; not noticed; occurs often.

1 m: slight to medium; low-lying coasts are flooded; occurs approximately once every four to eight months.

4 m: flooding; some damage to coastal buildings; lots of debris and litter; occurs approximately once a year.

8 m: very large; small buildings destroyed, large ones damaged; drownings; fish and sea mammals washed ashore; makes a roaring sound; occurs approximately once every three years.

16 m: disastrous; almost all buildings totally destroyed; trees uprooted; all ships badly damaged; many deaths and injuries; occurs approximately once every ten years.

The Asian tsunami of December 2004 fell into the last category. With waves reaching 15 metres in height as they hit land, this was one of the worst natural disasters in living memory – more than 220,000 people were killed almost instantly and it is estimated that a further 150,000 will die from disease in the wake of the disaster. Witnesses said they heard a sound like the roaring of a jet plane before the waves struck and whole communities were wiped out in a matter of seconds.

One reason for the extent of the damage is that no warning system exists in the Indian Ocean, where the undersea earthquake that caused the tsunami occurred. Ninety per cent of the world's really powerful tsunamis happen in the Pacific Ocean. This area is called the Pacific Ring of Fire (see page 29) because so many volcanoes and earthquakes happen here. There are plate margins all around the Pacific. Four hundred tsunamis occur here every year, though most are small. Japan and Taiwan are affected by about a quarter of these. Pacific tsunamis can travel at 800 kph and cross the whole ocean in less than a day.

Systems warning of an approaching tsunami have been operating in some parts of the Pacific Ocean since 1948. The Pacific Warning System is based in Honolulu in Hawaii and helps to warn 24 countries of approaching danger. Its 100 seismic and tidal stations are spread across the ocean. They try to give any area at risk at least one hour to prepare and evacuate. By the time scientists working here had registered the Asian tsunami, it was too late to begin proper evacuation procedures in the countries at risk.

Tsunami damage

There are three main ways in which tsunamis cause damage:
• Whole buildings can be picked up and moved inland. Sometimes they are pulled out to sea as the wave goes back (hydrostatic effects).
• Debris carried by the wave can be thrown at buildings and people, causing damage (shock effects).
• The shock of being hit by something so powerful smashes roads, bridges and harbours (hydrodynamic effects).

▼ This aerial view shows the waters of the tsunami receding from the coastal area of Kalutara in Sri Lanka. As the waters swirled back, they carried wreckage with them.

The Asian tsunami

On 26 December 2004, plate movement deep beneath the Indian Ocean triggered an earthquake off the coast of Sumatra. Measuring 9.0 on the Richter scale, the earthquake created huge amounts of energy that sent shockwaves out in all directions. The resulting tsunami sped across the ocean, gaining height as it approached land, and eventually crashed into coastlines all across Asia. Even Africa, 5,000 km from the epicentre, was affected. Many people were unaware of the danger they were in; some even rushed to the water's edge to see what was happening. People drowned and buildings and vehicles were destroyed as the waves enveloped coastal areas and then sucked the debris back out to sea.

Mountains of Fire

There are several types of volcano, and they are all shaped differently because of the various processes responsible for their formation. Despite having very different shapes and characteristics, all volcanoes have some features in common. Their sides may be built of different materials but they all have a vent – a hole in the middle where the magma comes up to the surface. Magma varies in its chemical composition and temperature, and both of these factors affect the size and shape of the volcano. Most volcanoes have a magma chamber, a large space underground where molten rock from the mantle collects. The pressure builds up and the magma pushes harder to break through the Earth's surface, until eventually it does so in a volcanic eruption. When magma reaches the surface it is called lava. Lava varies in temperature between 900°C and 1,200°C. The hotter the lava, the thinner and runnier it is, so the faster and further it flows.

Surtsey

The shield volcano Surtsey is located just off the south-west coast of Iceland, 18 km beyond Heimaey – another set of volcanic islands sitting on the Mid-Atlantic Ridge. Surtsey's eruption in 1963 built up this undersea volcano high enough from the ocean floor that it became one of the world's newest islands. Several eruptions happened one after the other, up to 1967. Having been formed so recently, it is one of the most filmed and most thoroughly researched places on Earth.

▶ Fissure volcanoes do not have a traditional dome shape; instead the lava erupts from huge cracks, or fissures, in the ground.

▶▶ Today Surtsey has an area of 3 km² and its highest point stands 150 metres above sea level. At first the area was a little larger, but the sea has eroded some of the less consolidated lava. Despite the fact that Surtsey continued to erupt for three years from 1963, plants were spotted there as early as 1964, their seeds having been carried by the wind and water, and dropped by birds.

Types of volcano

Fissure volcanoes hardly look like volcanoes at all. Their lava is so hot, thin and runny that it flows great distances and never builds up a cone-shaped hill. In other volcanoes, lava comes out through the vent, but in fissure volcanoes lava erupts through cracks in the ground – part of the plate boundary. The lava fills in any hollows, forming a smooth landscape.

Shield volcanoes are made of basic lava – hot, fast-flowing, runny lava with a temperature around 1,200°C. These volcanoes form on constructive plate boundaries or over hot spots in the middle of a plate. Iceland's volcanoes, such as Surtsey and Hekla, are examples of constructive-margin volcanoes. Mauna Loa, Mauna Kea and Kilauea on the Hawaiian islands are all hot-spot features.

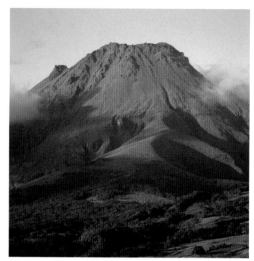

▲ Mount Pelée in the West Indies is an example of an acid dome volcano; the acidic lava that erupts from this volcano solidifies quickly, forming a steep-sided mountain.

Acidic lava is cooler than basic lava. It has a temperature of about 900°C. Solidifying quickly on contact with the air, this thick, sticky lava hardly flows any distance at all. Acid dome volcanoes therefore have a very distinctive shape, with narrow bases and steep sides. A spine forms at the top if lava solidifies so quickly it never gets out of the vent. Mount Pelée on Martinique in the West Indies is a famous lava dome.

Ash and cinder cones grow more quickly than any other type of volcano. Ash and cinders are both very light materials containing lots of air, so the symmetrical sides of these volcanoes build up quickly. Because they are not strong, however, they are easily weathered away in the few years after each eruption. Paracutin in Mexico grew to over 400 metres in its first eruption, which began with no warning in the middle of a farmer's cornfield in 1943.

Fissure volcano

▶ Base: Wide
▶ Sides: So gentle they can hardly be seen
▶ Example: Laki, Iceland

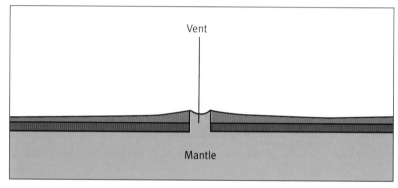

Shield volcano

▶ Base: Wide
▶ Sides: Gentle
▶ Example: Mauna Loa, Hawaii; Surtsey, Iceland

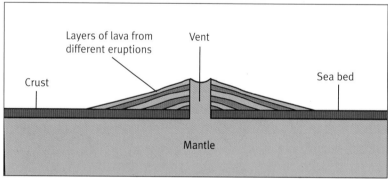

Acid dome volcano

▶ Base: Narrow
▶ Sides: Steep
▶ Example: Mount Pelée, Martinique

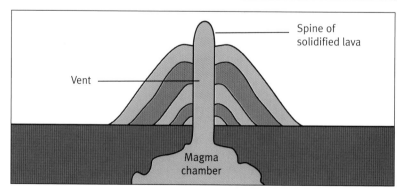

Composite volcanoes have alternate layers of acid lava and ash. As the lava erupts at the surface, the release of pressure causes the gases to come out with an explosion. This explosion turns the lava to ash, which flies high into the air and then falls on the volcano sides. Later the lava begins to flow, spreading down the volcano sides on top of the ash, making it stronger and less likely to erode over time. Composite volcanoes sometimes have additional vents and cones.

The most explosive volcanoes are calderas. The build-up of gases in the magma chamber and vent is so great that a huge explosion follows, blowing away the whole summit of the volcano. A large depression, called a caldera, is left behind. A caldera may contain a lake or be flooded by the sea.

▲ Mount St Helens, situated in Washington in the USA, is an example of a composite volcano. The volcano's lava is in the middle of the temperature range, so it flows for a moderate distance down the volcano sides before solidifying.

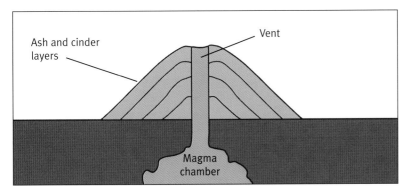

Ash and cinder volcano

▶ Base: Medium
▶ Sides: Moderately steep
▶ Example: Paracutin, Mexico

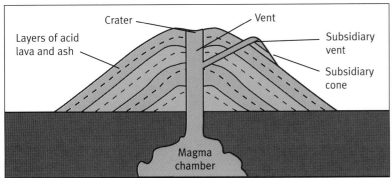

Composite volcano

▶ Base: Medium
▶ Sides: Moderately steep
▶ Example: Mount St Helens, USA

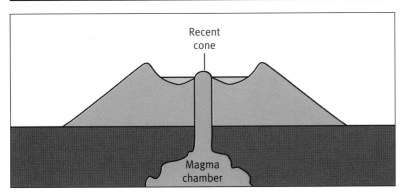

Caldera volcano

▶ Base: Medium
▶ Sides: Often cannot be distinguished
▶ Example: Krakatoa, Indonesia

Types of volcanic eruption

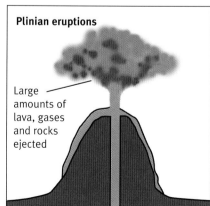

When Mount Vesuvius in Italy erupted in AD 79 it showered dust and ash over many kilometres. The entire city of Pompeii was buried in a matter of minutes and the inhabitants were effectively mummified and preserved where they were killed.

The most important factor affecting the type of eruption of any volcano is whether its lava is basic or acidic. Basic lava (high temperature and very fluid) appears at constructive plate boundaries and at hot spots in the middle of a plate. Acidic lava (low temperature and thick) erupts at destructive margins. There are many types of volcanic eruption; the five most varied examples are described below.

Icelandic and Hawaiian eruptions both involve basic lava. This means that the eruptions are relatively quiet, without explosions or great disruption to people. In an Icelandic eruption, lava flows gently from a fissure. Laki in Iceland is the best example, hence the name given to this type of eruption. Hawaiian eruptions are similar, except that the lava comes out of a vent at the centre of the volcano, rather than from a long crack in the ground. All the volcanoes in the American state of Hawaii are over hot spots and are of this type.

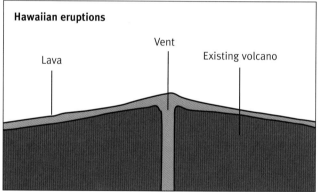

Icelandic and Hawaiian eruptions involve basic (alkaline) lava. There are thin layers of lava, widely spread and moving gently, and with little steam or other gases.

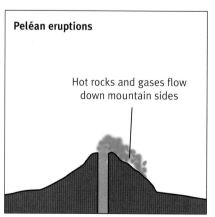

Krakatoan, Peléan and Plinian eruptions involve acidic lava. There is less lava, but more pyroclastic flow and they are very explosive.

▲ This illustration shows the nuée ardente – the massive cloud of hot gas and rocks – that destroyed St Pierre, the capital of Martinique, during the eruption of Mount Pelée in 1902.

Krakatoan, Peléan and Plinian eruptions all involve acidic lava. Krakatoan eruptions are exceptionally violent events. Much of the existing volcano can be exploded away each time the volcano erupts. They therefore never grow to be huge features in the landscape, but their wide, open shape is distinctive. Krakatoa in Indonesia, after which this type of eruption is named, and Crater Lake in the western USA, are both examples of volcanoes that erupt in this way.

Peléan eruptions are named after Mount Pelée in Martinique in the West Indies, which erupted in 1902. During this eruption, hardly any lava was involved, but the pyroclastic flows and nuées ardentes that resulted caused severe damage. Super-hot, dense gases flowed downhill with terrific speed, picking up and carrying rocks and other debris along the way, burning everything in their path.

Plinian eruptions are unusual. Named after the Roman author Pliny the Younger, who recorded the eruption of Mount Vesuvius that destroyed Pompeii in AD 79, they are probably the most violent of all volcanic eruptions. They produce large amounts of lava and pyroclastic materials. Dust, ash and volcanic bombs are flung higher into the air than with any other eruption. For this reason, they are the most dangerous.

● Mount Pelée

Mount Pelée is part of the island arc that makes up the Lesser Antilles of the Caribbean. It has erupted five times in the last 500 years: in 1635, 1792, 1851–52, 1902–05 and 1929–32. The eruption of 8 May 1902 destroyed the capital city, St Pierre, as the huge pyroclastic flow poured down the mountainside, destroying everything in its path. Nearly 30,000 people died – the largest number of casualties in a twentieth-century eruption. Most of the destruction was caused by a nuée ardente, a hot, glowing cloud of gas carrying solid particles. The gases engulfed everything within a few metres of the ground.

Hot spots

Hot spots are areas on one of the Earth's plates where hot rock bubbles up from the mantle. As the plate moves, the hot spot remains in the same place and keeps burning through the crust. This results in the formation of a chain of extinct volcanoes.

The impact of volcanoes

Volcanoes are found in every continent and many countries are affected by volcanic eruptions. MEDCs are better able to deal with the aftermath of an eruption; they also have the technology available to monitor active volcanoes and to forecast possible eruptions. Also, in most of these countries fewer people are forced to live on the sides of volcanoes in the risk zone, because population pressure is less severe. Three factors dictate the scale of the impact: the explosiveness of the eruption; how many people live in the danger area; and how developed the country is.

The Hawaiian volcanoes lie in the USA, which is an MEDC. These shield volcanoes erupt gently, so they pose limited danger to life and property. Mauna Loa, Mauna Kea and Kilauea are all peaks in this group of volcanic islands that lie over a hot spot in the Pacific Ocean.

Laki

Laki, in Iceland, is the best-known fissure volcano in the world. During the 1783 eruption, large amounts of sulphur gases were thrown out along with the lava. These gases are poisonous and very dangerous because they mix with oxygen and water vapour from the atmosphere to make – amongst other products – sulphuric acid. When the acidic vapour was washed out of the air by the rain, it killed many of the plants on the ground and poisoned the soil for several years. Crops would not grow and livestock perished. Over a ten-year period 40,000 Icelanders died of starvation because their livelihoods had been destroyed.

▶ When fissure volcanoes like Laki in Iceland erupt, they eject rivers of thin, runny lava through cracks in the ground. They never build up into the cone shape normally associated with volcanoes.

The Nyiragongo volcano lies in the Democratic Republic of Congo (East Central Africa), part of a chain of volcanoes along the Great East African Rift Valley. It erupted on 17 January 2002 and severely affected the city of Goma. Even though the only material ejected was lava, which flowed relatively slowly (rather like Mauna Loa), the town was utterly devastated. Homes and other buildings were destroyed, roads were blocked, jobs were lost and crops were destroyed. Half a million people were displaced. Because Congo is an LEDC, and because it is very remote and in a rainforest zone, help arrived very slowly. The situation was compounded when lava flowed over the airport runways, preventing supplies being flown in. Congo has few people trained to cope with emergencies and little equipment available. In many LEDCs people are not insured against such disasters, so they have to start again from scratch. Nyiragongo continues to erupt, though quite gently, which makes it difficult for people to restart their lives.

▲ Mauna Loa's summit is 8 km above its base on the Pacific Ocean floor. It makes up half the island of Hawaii and it has been forming for almost one million years. It is one of the most active volcanoes on Earth, having erupted 35 times since the early 1800s. The last eruption was in 1984.

The Pacific Ring of Fire

The Pacific Ring of Fire is so named because this ocean is ringed by numerous volcanoes. Almost all the plate margins around the Pacific are destructive, so volcanoes are common. Only a few sections, like the San Andreas Fault in California, consist of plate boundaries without volcanoes. There are even volcanoes located within the Pacific, such as those that form the Hawaiian islands; these are located over hot spots in the Earth's crust. The Pacific is the most volcanically active region in the world, and some of the most famous volcanoes can be found in this region.

▶ Some of the best-known volcanoes in the world are part of the Pacific Ring of Fire. These include Mount Fuji in Japan, Mount Pinatubo in the Philippines and Mount St Helens in the USA. The orange ring on the map marks the concentration of volcanoes around the plates.

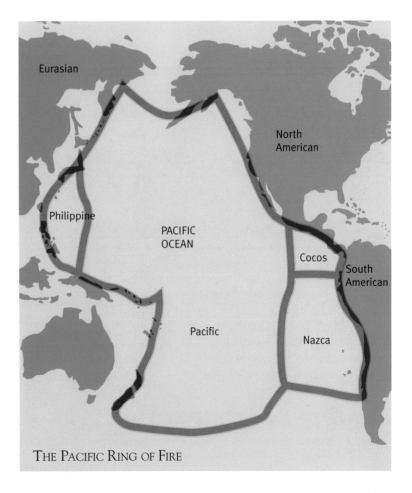

THE PACIFIC RING OF FIRE

Effects on the landscape

On 18 May 1980 an eruption blew the top off Mount St Helens, a volcano in Washington state, USA. Before the eruption, the landscape of this area was considered so beautiful it had been made a National Park. When the volcano erupted, this pristine, forested landscape was turned into a wasteland in just a few minutes.

During the early moments of the eruption, heat from the pyroclastic surge melted snow and ice on the mountaintop. Huge, destructive floods swept down the valleys, and the water mixed with soil, creating volcanic mudflows called lahars. Homes, roads, bridges and trees were all washed away. The landscape was totally altered.

▼ The eruption of Mount St Helens in the USA in 1980 was one of the worst volcanic eruptions of the twentieth century. Its effects were felt for hundreds of kilometres over the surrounding area.

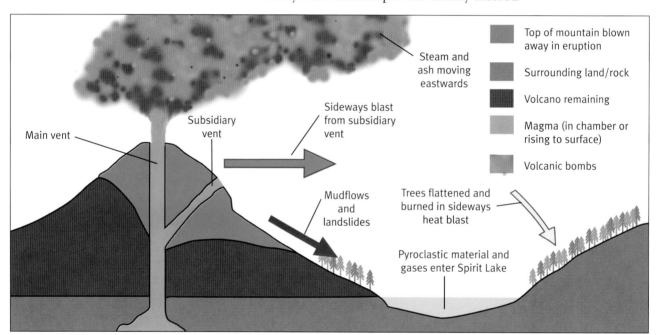

Main vent

Subsidiary vent

Steam and ash moving eastwards

Sideways blast from subsidiary vent

Mudflows and landslides

Trees flattened and burned in sideways heat blast

Pyroclastic material and gases enter Spirit Lake

Top of mountain blown away in eruption

Surrounding land/rock

Volcano remaining

Magma (in chamber or rising to surface)

Volcanic bombs

On the volcano itself, the northern side of the mountain was shaken loose, causing a massive rock avalanche. The debris was spread over 600 km². Almost 400 metres were blown off the mountain's height. The cone shape of the top of the mountain was opened up into a wide crater.

The huge explosion from the subsidiary vent sent a shock wave of immensely hot gases sideways at 300–500 kph, flattening trees within the blast zone and incinerating the leaves, needles and twigs of those further away. Spirit Lake, which had been an important place for fishing and other recreation, was filled in with mud, rocks and other debris.

Lots of ash fell into it and poisonous gases from the blast were dissolved in its water, making it very acidic. All its wildlife died.

A huge amount of ash was released by this Plinian eruption, turning the landscape a uniform shade of grey. The ash cloud spread eastwards, ruining crops. Car engines were damaged. Visibility was so bad it was like being in a thick fog.

Scientists have been amazed at the speed with which plants and animals return after volcanic eruptions. Ash, when weathered, is quite fertile and plants can take root in it. Eventually even dense vegetation returns. Smaller, hardy plants capable of surviving in difficult conditions with poor soil begin the process by colonising the area. Gradually conditions improve – the soil becomes deeper and more fertile – and new plants start to grow as seeds are blown in from the surrounding area. In the case of Mount St Helens, people helped the process, too. Ten million trees were replanted.

▼ An aerial view of the eruption of Mount St Helens in 1980.

Positive aspects of volcanic eruptions

Much about volcanic eruptions is destructive and negative, but this is not the whole story. Volcanoes can bring huge benefits to people living near them. The two main ways are agriculture and tourism. People can make their living out of both of these economic activities.

Some parts of the world have a severe shortage of agricultural land. Countries consisting of several small islands and which have a high population – such as Indonesia – are always short of land for producing food. Volcanic lava undergoes weathering to form extremely rich soils. In a country where land is in short supply, such soils are very valuable.

Volcanic landscapes are incredibly beautiful, so people are prepared to travel to see them. Several have a thriving tourist industry. When Mount St Helens showed signs of erupting in spring 1980, many people flocked to watch it happen, not realising the dangers. Some were killed. Walkers, climbers and water-sports enthusiasts had regularly visited this area because it was so attractive.

▲ Volcanoes can be huge tourist attractions, which can be important for the economy of a region. Here, tourists follow a trail to the volcanic peaks on Bartolome Island in Ecuador.

▼ To make the best use of the land available, people in countries like Indonesia construct terraces in the rich soil on the sides of volcanoes.

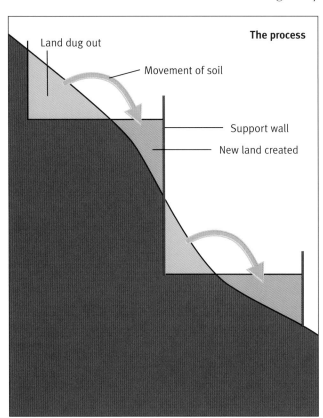

The process

Land dug out

Movement of soil

Support wall

New land created

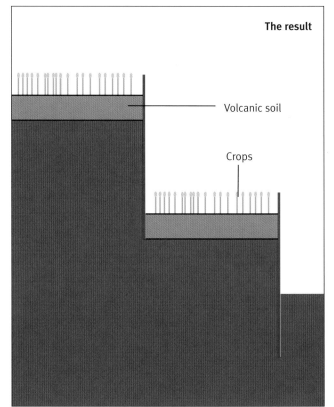

The result

Volcanic soil

Crops

Geysers are a feature of some volcanic areas. Water is heated underground and explodes out at the surface. Old Faithful in the USA is probably the best-known geyser in the world. Millions of people visit it every year. The special attraction of Old Faithful is that it spurts regularly, every 80 minutes, up to a height of 57 metres, lasting between one and five minutes each time.

Fumaroles are jets of steam that appear at the surface close to some volcanoes, where the crust can be as thin as 3 metres. Steam and sulphurous gases are emitted through cracks in the ground. Other hydrothermal phenomena are hot springs. New Zealand's South Island has these, along with hot mud pools that are said to have health-giving properties.

Some volcanic areas exploit cheap natural energy. Iceland uses geothermal energy. Underground water is heated by the magma and this provides the whole of Reykjavik, Iceland's capital, with very cheap heating for homes and other buildings. Even tropical crops such as bananas can be grown in greenhouses heated by this volcanic resource.

▲ Geysers like Old Faithful in Yellowstone National Park in the USA consist of deep wells in fissures in the rock. The water in the well is heated by the surrounding rocks until it suddenly boils and erupts.

◀ These greenhouses in Iceland are heated using geothermal energy, an environmentally friendly form of energy. It is readily available in Iceland because of the geological activity caused by the country's position on a plate boundary.

The Effects of Earthquakes and Volcanoes

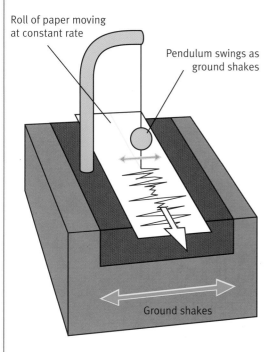

Roll of paper moving at constant rate

Pendulum swings as ground shakes

Ground shakes

▲ In a pendulum seismograph, the pendulum swings as the ground shakes. A roll of paper moves steadily (white arrow) beneath a pen, which records the earthquake waves. The broader the sweep, the more intense the earthquake.

▲ These seismographs are situated at the Parkfield laboratory in California, where seismologists predict and prepare for earthquakes that might hit the region.

In the parts of the world where volcanic eruptions and earthquakes take place, people live with the constant threat that their homes and land could be destroyed. In many countries, the occurrences of both earthquakes and volcanic eruptions can be predicted and measures taken to prevent large-scale loss of life. Other countries, however, are not so well-equipped.

Seismology and the prediction of earthquakes

Seismology is the study and measurement of earthquakes. It is the main tool used today for learning more about earthquakes in the hope of predicting when and where they may occur. Earthquakes are recorded using instruments called seismographs.

Even early seismographs were quite sensitive. The earliest known piece of equipment was invented by Choko, in China, in AD 136. His seismograph consisted of a copper vessel with eight dragon-head shapes attached to it, each with a ball in its mouth. Underneath each head was a metal frog with its mouth turned upwards. During the shaking of an earthquake, some, or all, of the balls would drop from the dragons' into the frogs' mouths. The number of balls falling, and the pattern of those that fell, showed the strength and position of the earthquake. More recently, scientists have used a pendulum seismograph.

Modern seismology has provided much information about the Earth's interior. Seismic tomography is an imaging method similar to that used in making CAT scans (X-rays of the brain). The Parkfield research centre in the USA is run by the USGS (United States Geological Survey) and is developing equipment that will pick up the slightest movements, from which we may be able to predict earthquakes in the future. The most up-to-date equipment is digital and uses broadband. It can sense even very slight movement, and works over a large range of frequencies. Rather than a pendulum moving, this equipment records the amount of energy needed to keep something still during the shaking.

Modern monitoring methods

Laser reflector: Detects small amounts of movement along a fault.

Ordinary surveying equipment: Used to see whether the level of land has changed on either side of a fault.

Tiltmeter: Detects minor changes in the angle of the ground.

Gravity meter/magnetometer: Detects changes in the local magnetic field.

Radon gas counter: The amount of radon gas dissolved in underground water can increase before an earthquake.

Seismographs located underground: Used to pick up any foreshocks underground.

Strainmeter: Used to measure the stresses in the rocks.

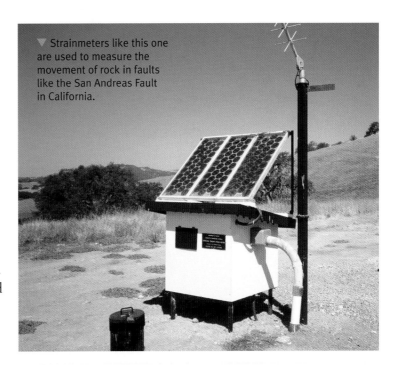

▼ Strainmeters like this one are used to measure the movement of rock in faults like the San Andreas Fault in California.

The Morocco earthquake

An earthquake struck Morocco on 25 February 2004. The powerful earthquake measured 6.5 on the Richter scale and killed nearly 600 people. In Al Hoceima city, modern central city buildings had been constructed to withstand earthquakes. However, the poorer suburbs were severely affected as their lower-quality homes collapsed. Some of the worst-hit places were remote inland villages in the Rif mountains. Traditional mud huts in Tazaghin were completely flattened by the ground shaking.

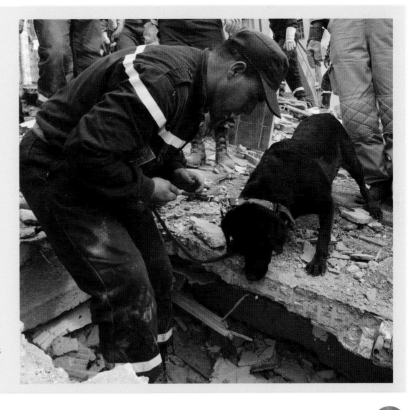

▶ Rescuers use dogs to try to locate survivors buried under the rubble after the Moroccan earthquake in February 2004.

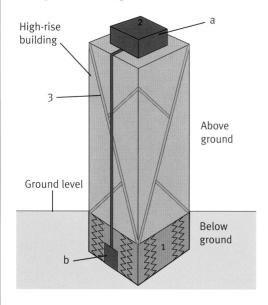

▼ Aseismic designs include: 1) rubber shock absorbers in the foundations to allow a building to shake safely; 2) concrete weights at the top of the building (a) can be controlled by computers in the basement (b) and can be moved to balance the strain on the building; 3) cross-bracings to reduce damage to the building.

High-rise building

3

a

Above ground

Ground level

Below ground

b

Living with earthquakes

There are two main ways to make living in an earthquake zone safer: preventing damage by making buildings safer, and keeping people safe after an earthquake. Collapsing buildings are responsible for most deaths, but an aseismic design makes buildings less likely to fall. As a rule, taller buildings are more dangerous, but the proportions of the structure are also important. Buildings do not just shake during an earthquake – they can twist too. Many countries now have strict building regulations and newer buildings are much safer than older ones. Every earthquake gives engineers more information on which designs are the most effective.

No matter how clever the designs of earthquake-proof buildings become, there will always be mess to clear up and rescue work to do following an earthquake, as well as simple survival in difficult conditions. The Californian state government encourages people to have the right

● The emergency services

The work of the emergency services after an earthquake needs very careful organisation. The right people and equipment must be in the right place at the right time. This can be difficult when roads and telephones are disrupted.

The Tokyo Gas Company overcomes this problem by using a radio network communication system. This can tell the central computer about pipeline damage. 'Smart meters' automatically cut off gas in an earthquake measuring more than 5 on the Richter scale.

In California, computer systems are being developed to keep the emergency services constantly up to date. The 'Readicube' system will mean they know within five seconds of an earthquake exactly where they are needed.

Workplaces and schools already operate earthquake drills so people know how to evacuate and are able to do a lot for themselves without the emergency services.

◀ In areas like California, where earthquakes are a frequent occurrence, earthquake drills are operated so everybody – even schoolchildren – knows what to do in an emergency.

equipment readily available in an emergency. This includes sturdy shoes and heavy gloves to help with rescue work, a garden hose to help with fire fighting, a change of clothing, a tent, candles and matches.

Safe food and water supplies are perhaps most important for survival. Disease can be a killer after an earthquake. One gallon of water per person per day is required. Cooking may have to be outside and camping stoves will be useful. Food needs to be dried, such as cereals and energy bars, or in cans, because it keeps without a fridge. A minimum of three days' worth of food is recommended. Large refuse sacks to dispose of waste are needed, too.

Predicting a volcanic eruption – Mount Pinatubo

Mount Pinatubo lies on the island of Luzon, the most northerly of the larger islands of the Philippines. Situated on a destructive margin between the Philippine and Eurasian plates, this is one of the most active volcanic areas in the world. Pinatubo's most recent eruption, which began on 15 June 1991, was its first real activity for 400 years, but it proved to be the biggest eruption anywhere on Earth in the twentieth century.

Due to the high volcanic risk in the Philippines, the country's volcanoes are constantly monitored by geologists and volcanologists who work together in PHIVOLCS (the Philippine Institute of Volcanology and Seismology), an organisation funded by the government. They are helped by the USGS.

Before the eruption in 1991, several pieces of equipment were already in place on and around Mount Pinatubo. Tiltmeters were located on all the Philippine volcanoes. These show any change in the angle of the ground and allow volcanologists to measure the development of the bulge on the side of the volcano prior to its eruption, and to evacuate the area in time. Seismographs were also used on Pinatubo. Volcanoes often shake as the pressure in the magma chamber below builds up and magma forces its way up the vent. Geologists monitoring Pinatubo noticed signs of such a build-up weeks before the actual eruption.

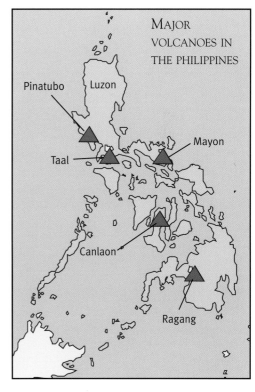

▲ The volcanoes in the Philippines are known to have the potential to erupt with tremendous force. Even though Pinatubo had not been active for four centuries, other Filipino volcanoes, such as Mayon, further south-east on Luzon, had been, so scientists already had some precautionary equipment in place.

This radar image of Mount Pinatubo shows how far the ash spread from the 1991 eruption (marked in red). The wide black channels leading from the volcano are mud deposits.

Geologists use a standard hazard-warning system to assess whether evacuation is necessary and when that will be:

Level 1: Steam comes out of the ground; tiny earthquakes are picked up on the monitoring equipment.
Level 2: Continuous steam and gas emissions; some regular earthquake activity.
Level 3: Greatly increased earthquake activity; volcanic shaking starts.
Level 4: Dome of viscous magma appears; more earthquakes and tremors; ash emissions.
Level 5: First large explosive eruption; ash output increasing quickly.

It is often difficult to decide when, if at all, people should be evacuated from an area. If the 'safe' decision is taken and people are evacuated but no event occurs, unnecessary disruption has been caused, and there is the risk that in the future the geologists will not be believed. If the decision to evacuate is left too late and the volcano erupts, severe damage to property and loss of life may occur. In the case of Pinatubo, the scientists made the right decision and ordered an evacuation. Local people picked up their belongings and walked away. Although there were still deaths, many of these were caused by lahars triggered by the torrential rains that came with the monsoon. The situation could have been much worse.

Geologists carefully monitor volcanic activity, including gas emissions, in order to work out whether or not to evacuate an area.

Pinatubo statistics

- 5 billion m³ of ash and other pyroclastic materials ejected
- Eruption column 18 km wide and 30 km high
- Dust and ash in the air went around the whole world in the upper atmosphere
- Global temperatures initially dropped by 3°C
- Global temperatures lower by 1°C on average for three years
- 740 dead
- 184 injured
- 23 missing, bodies never found
- Over one million homeless

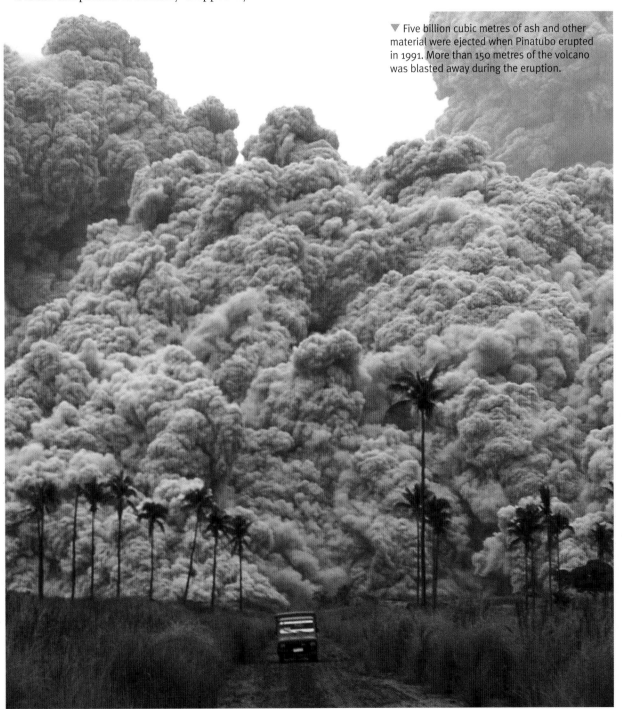

▼ Five billion cubic metres of ash and other material were ejected when Pinatubo erupted in 1991. More than 150 metres of the volcano was blasted away during the eruption.

Armero

In 1985 the town of Armero in Colombia (an LEDC) experienced a huge volcanic disaster. Lying on a subduction zone between the Nazca and South American plates, the eruption of the Nevado del Ruiz volcano was moderately explosive, but few people lived close enough to be directly affected. However, snow and ice lying over the mountain melted. Water mixed with soil and debris to create a huge mudslide, which destroyed everything in its path. Armero, lying down-valley from the volcano, suffered its full force. It happened during the night, so people were unable to see the hazard approaching. Armero's survivors eventually moved on, unable to live with the physical and emotional destruction the volcano had caused.

▶ The town of Armero in Colombia was destroyed by the mudflows that resulted from the eruption of the Nevado del Ruiz volcano – 23,000 people died in the disaster.

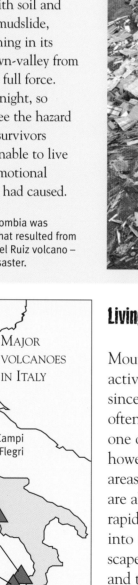

MAJOR VOLCANOES IN ITALY

Campi Flegri

Vesuvius

Strombi

Vulcano

Etna

Living with volcanoes - Mount Etna

Mount Etna is Europe's highest (3,200 metres) and most active volcano and its eruptions have been documented since 1,500 BC. Etna has erupted 200 times since then, often close to settlements. Volcanic soil makes this area one of the most fertile in the whole of the Mediterranean; however, Etna's frequent eruptions threaten cultivated areas, homes and even whole settlements. As more people are able to travel, the local tourist industry has grown rapidly in recent years and it brings a great deal of money into the area. Tourists come to see the spectacular landscape, hot lava, the bubbling activity within the crater and the colourful pyroclastic displays. The volcano gives lots of opportunities to view nature's fireworks.

In fact, the chance of a person living near Etna ever having their home engulfed by lava is very small. Etna's acidic lava flows sufficiently slowly that it is possible to get out of its way. The main impact takes the form of small falls of ash or grit-sized fragments. Sometimes individual buildings are damaged or destroyed. In the past, however, Etna has experienced cataclysmic eruptions. Major eruptions happened in the years 1169 and 1669, exactly 500 years apart. If the same time gap continues between eruptions, the next one would be due in 2169.

In many cases the advantages of living in these fertile regions outweighs the risks. As understanding of volcanoes and seismic activity grows, people can lead their lives more confidently in the shadows of volcanoes.

▼ A volcanologist wearing a heat-proof suit, on the solidified lava around Mount Etna in Italy. In 2001 Etna began to pour out its lava flows once again, with 16 separate eruptions. Five vents produced thick lava with lots of steam and smoke. The town of Nicolosi was especially under threat and lava movement was monitored closely.

Glossary

acid dome volcano A volcano with a steep-sided body; solidified lava blocks the vent of the volcano, making the top section higher and possibly wider.

acid lava Thick, sticky, slow-flowing lava with a temperature between 900°C and 1,200°C.

aseismic Any engineering method that makes a building more resistant to earthquake damage.

ash and cinder cone A volcano with explosive eruptions of ash but little or no lava; easily eroded because its material is not very resistant.

basalt A dark-coloured igneous rock, often found in oceanic plates or in the material welling up at constructive plate margins.

basic lava Thin, fast-flowing lava with a temperature higher than 1,200°C.

caldera A large volcanic crater formed by the collapse of the cone of a volcano during a very explosive eruption.

collision zone A plate boundary where two continental plates move towards each other.

composite volcano A volcano made of alternate layers of ash and lava; it may have side (subsidiary) vents and cones.

cone One of the simplest volcano formations, built by fragments (ejecta) ejected from a volcanic vent, piling up around the vent in the shape of a cone with a central crater.

conservative boundary A boundary where two plates are sliding past each other, sometimes getting stuck and causing earthquakes when they jolt free.

constructive boundary A boundary where two plates are moving apart and new crust is created.

continental crust Parts of the Earth's crust composed of light rocks. They are made of compounds containing lots of silica (sand) and aluminium.

continental drift The theory by Alfred Wegener explaining why the Earth's continents appear to move and split into different sections.

convection current A current of hot magma in the mantle. It rises from the lower part of the mantle, where temperatures are hottest, towards the crust.

core The central part of the Earth, made of iron and nickel.

crater The top section of the vent of a volcano, usually blocked by solidified lava between eruptions.

crust The outermost layer of the Earth.

destructive boundary A boundary at which two plates are moving towards each other. The denser plate dips down below the other and melts.

earthquake lights Unexplained flashes of light that appear just before or during an earthquake, usually lasting a few seconds each time.

epicentre The point on the Earth's surface vertically above the focus, where the worst damage usually occurs in an earthquake.

fault A fracture in the Earth's crust that displaces the rocks on either side of it.

fissure A huge crack in the ground, often part of a plate boundary.

fissure volcano A volcano in which lava erupts along the fissure and is able to flow far from the vent.

focus The point underground from which an earthquake originates.

fold mountains Mountains made of a set of parallel ridges caused when the continental rocks 'pile up' at a destructive boundary or collision zone.

fumarole A vent from which volcanic vapours escape, from the Latin *fumariolum*, a smoke-hole.

geothermal Energy that may be generated by the utilisation of naturally occurring geological heat sources. It is a form of renewable energy.

geyser A natural underground stream that throws out hot water and jets of steam from the ground.

hot spot An area on the Earth's surface where the crust is quite thin. Magma can break through and form a volcano.

hydrodynamic effect The smashing of structures such as roads or bridges by a tsunami.

hydrostatic event When buildings and other structures are forced inland or pulled back into the sea by a tsunami.

hydrothermal Relating to water heated underground by volcanic activity.

intra-plate A point within a plate not near its edges.

island arc A chain of islands formed when volcanoes created on the ocean floor grow tall enough to break the surface.

L waves Longitudinal waves; earthquake waves that begin as P or S waves but then move along the Earth's surface.

lahar A kind of mudslide made of volcanic materials and water.

lava Magma when it has broken through the Earth's surface.

LEDC Less Economically Developed Country; these countries usually have poorer communications and emergency services and suffer more severely from the effects of earthquakes and volcanoes.

magma Molten rock in the Earth's mantle.

magma chamber The space beneath a volcano in which the magma is held before an eruption.

mantle The layer of the Earth above the core and beneath the crust.

MEDC More Economically Developed Country; these countries are usually better prepared for the consequences of earthquakes and volcanoes.

Mercalli scale A scale to measure the damage done by earthquakes. It is not connected to the energy of the earthquake. If there is more settlement in an area there is likely to be more damage, so the level is higher.

Mid-Atlantic Ridge The name given to the mid-ocean ridge stretching down the centre of the Atlantic Ocean.

mudflow Mud and sediment saturated with water and moving rapidly downhill or in a channel. Also called a lahar.

nuée ardente A cloud of extremely hot gas that 'rolls' down the side of an erupting volcano.

oceanic crust Parts of the Earth's crust made of denser rocks.

P waves Primary or 'push' waves; earthquake waves that travel from the epicentre up to the surface of the Earth.

plate A section of the Earth's crust.

plate tectonics The theory developed in the 1960s from earlier ideas of continental drift. It explains the nature of the Earth's plates, the way they move and the features that form at their boundaries, including earthquakes and volcanoes.

pyroclastic flow Volcanic ash, dust, bombs and other fragments in hot, dense gases, which roll downhill at high speed.

Richter sale A scale for measuring the energy or magnitude of an earthquake.

S waves Secondary or 'shake' waves; earthquake waves that travel away from epicentre.

seismic waves Movements in the Earth's crust that indicate that an earthquake may be about to happen or is already happening.

seismogram The printout from a seismograph.

seismograph Equipment used to measure the amount of ground shaking associated with an earthquake or volcano.

seismologist A scientist or geologist who studies earthquakes.

shield volcano A wide-based volcano with basic, runny lava.

shock effects When debris carried by a tsunami damages buildings and kills or injures people.

subduction zone A destructive plate boundary where a dense oceanic plate is forced down below a lighter continental one, where it melts.

tsunami A large wave caused by an undersea earthquake or volcanic eruption.

USGS United States Geological Survey – the main group of scientists working on volcanoes and earthquakes, their prediction and prevention, throughout the world.

vent The hollow central part of a volcano, out of which lava, steam and other materials are ejected.

volcanologist A scientist or geologist who studies volcanoes and their behaviour.

weathering The wearing away of rock by rain, frost, plant roots and animals burrowing.

Further Information

Books

Amazing Planet Earth by John Farndon et al: Southwater, 2001

Earth-Shattering Earthquakes by Anita Ganeri: Scholastic Hippo, 2000

Hazards and Responses by Victoria Bishop: HarperCollins Publishers, 2001

The Kingfisher Geography Encyclopedia by Clive Gifford: Kingfisher Publications, 2003

Violent Volcanoes by Anita Ganeri: Scholastic Hippo, 1999

Volcano by Lisa Magloff: Eye Wonder Series, Dorling Kindersley, 2003

Volcanoes and Earthquakes by Rebecca Hunter: Discovering Geography Series, Raintree, 2004

Web sites

http:// www.eri.u-tokyo.ac.jp/
The web site for the Earthquake Research Institute at the University of Tokyo, which contains all the latest development in the prediction of and preparation for earthquakes.

http://www.pbs.org/wnet/savageearth/
Learn about the Earth's major tectonic plates and the natural hazards caused by their movement such as earthquakes and volcanoes.

http://www.phivolcs.dost.gov.ph/
Home page of the Philippine Institute of Volcanology and Seismology, with information about earthquakes and volcanoes.

http://www.usgs.gov/
Home page of the US Geological Survey, with vast amounts of resources and news stories about the geography and geology of the United States, including information and updates about earthquakes and volcanoes.

http://www.volcanolive.com/
A site packed with links to information on all aspects of volcanoes and volcanic activity, including maps of the world's volcanoes and how to deal with disasters caused by them.

Index

45

Acknowledgements

About the author

Alison Rae has been writing articles and books for over ten years, covering a range of geographical subjects, from physical hazards and studies of ecosystems to environmental issues and human impact on landscape features. She is editor for the successful online Geofile series as well as contributing articles to the publication, including 'The Iceland Volcano – A Multiple Hazard' and 'Recent Earthquakes and Volcanoes'. She has also contributed to the Geographical Association's teacher materials and the GeoActive series.

About the consultant

Simon Ross is Head of Geography at Queen's College in Taunton, Somerset. He has published extensively on all aspects of physical geography, from introductory level to upper secondary. His books include *Natural Hazards*, *Introducing Physical Geography and Map Reading*, and several books in the series Geography 21. He has worked as editor on many series, including Longman Co-Ordinated Geography and Longman Exploring Geography. He has also acted as consultant on television programmes for the BBC, and for the QCA on Geography Key Stage 3 resources. He regularly lectures and contributes articles to encyclopedias and journals.

Picture Credits

Cover: (t) Krafft/ Explorer/Science Photo Library **(bl)** Peter Menzel/Science Photo Library **(br)** Professor Stewart Lowther/ Science Photo Library **6** Krafft/Explorer/Science Photo Library **7(t)** Peter Menzel/Science Photo Library **7(b)** Adam G. Sylvester/ Science Photo Library **9(b)** Krafft/Hoa-Qui/Science Photo Library **11(t)** © Galen Rowell/Corbis **12(l)** James King-Holmes/Science Photo Library **13(t)** Peter Menzel/Science Photo Library **14(t)** © Wolfgang Rattay/Reuters/Corbis **14(b)** © Bettmann/ Corbis **15(t)** Joe Pasieka/Science Photo Library **15(b)** NASA/ Science Photo Library **16** © PBNJ Productions/ Corbis **17** Jean-Loup Charmet/Science Photo Library **18** © Reuters/Corbis **19(t)** © Bettmann/Corbis **19(b)** Lynette Cook/Science Photo Library **20(b)** © Lloyd Cluff/Corbis **21** © Romeo Ranoco/ Reuters/Corbis **22** Courtesy of Digital Globe **23** © Pierre Vauthey/Corbis Sygma **24(t)** © James L. Amos/ Corbis **25(t)** Professor Stewart Lowther/Science Photo Library **26(t)** © Bettmann/Corbis **27(t)** David Hardy/Science Photo Library **28** David Hardy/Science Photo Library **29(t)** NASA/ Science Photo Library **31** NASA/Science Photo Library **32(t)** © Kevin Schafer/Corbis **33(t)** David Halpern/Science Photo Library **33(b)** Martin Bond/Science Photo Library **34(b)** Peter Menzel/ Science Photo Library **35(t)** David Parker/Science Photo Library **35(b)** © Andrea Comas/Reuters/ Corbis **36(b)** David Parker/ Science Photo Library **38(t)** NASA/Science Photo Library **38(b)** British Antarctic Survey/Science Photo Library **39** © Alberto Garcia/Corbis **40(t)** © Jacques Languevin/Corbis **41** Jeremy Bishop/Science Photo Library